First published in Great Britain in 1997 by
BROCKHAMPTON PRESS,
a member of the Hodder Headline Group,
20 Bloomsbury Street, London WC1B 3QA.

This series of little gift books was made by Frances Banfield, Penny Clarke,
Clive Collins, Jack Cooper, Nick Diggory, John Dunne, David Goodman, Paul Gregory,
Douglas Hall, Lucinda Hawksley, Dicky Howett, Dennis Hovell, Helen Johnson,
C. M. Lee, John Maxwell, Patrick McCreeth, Morse Modaberi, Sonya Newland,
Anne Newman, Terry Price, Mike Seabrook, Nigel Soper, Karen Sullivan,
Nick Wells and Matt Weyland.

Compilation and selection copyright © 1997 Brockhampton Press.

All rights reserved. No part of this publication may be reproduced,
stored in a retrieval system, or transmitted in any form or by any means,
without the prior written permission of the copyright holder.

ISBN 1 86019 562 8

A copy of the CIP data is available from the British Library upon request.

Produced for Brockhampton Press by
Flame Tree Publishing, a part of The Foundry Creative Media Company Limited,
The Long House, Antrobus Road, Chiswick, London W4 5HY.

Printed and bound in Italy by L.E.G.O. Spa.

THE LITTLE BOOK OF
Cherubs

Selected by Karen Sullivan

BROCKHAMPTON PRESS

THE LITTLE BOOK OF CHERUBS

THE LITTLE BOOK OF CHERUBS

It is not because angels are holier than men or devils that makes them angels, but because they do not expect holiness from one another, but from God only.

William Blake

There are nine angelic orders,
and cherubim are up there in the highest choir.

Anonymous

And I heard a voice from heaven,
as the voice of many waters,
and as the voice of a great thunder:
and I heard the voice of harpers
harping with their harps.

Revelation, XIV:2

...I think, this passionate sigh, which half-begun
I stifle back, may reach and stir the plumes
Of God's calm angel standing in the sun.

Elizabeth Barrett Browning

The Angels were all singing out of tune,
And hoarse with having little else to do,
Excepting to wind up the sun and moon
Or curb a runaway young star or two.

Lord Byron, 'The Vision of Judgement'

Make friends with the angels, who though invisible are always with you... Often invoke them, constantly praise them, and make good use of their help and assistance in all your temporal and spiritual affairs.

Saint Francis de Sales

Angels may be very excellent sort of folk in their own way, but we, poor mortals in our present state, would probably find them precious slow company.

Jerome K. Jerome

Those who consider the Devil to be a partisan of Evil and angels to be warriors for Good accept the demagogy of the angels.
Things are clearly more complicated.

Milan Kundera

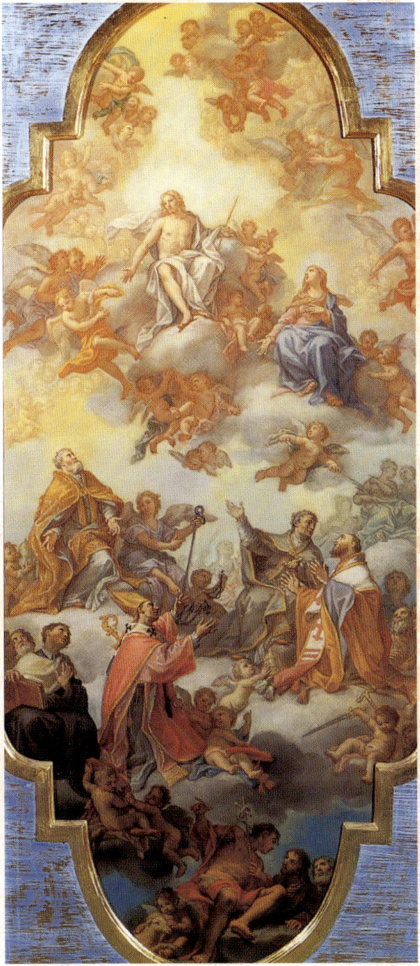

THE LITTLE BOOK OF CHERUBS

What angel wakes me from my flow'ry bed?

William Shakespeare, *A Midsummer Night's Dream*

Whither shall I go from thy spirit?
Or whither shall I flee from thy presence?
If I ascend up into heaven, thou art there:
if I make my bed in hell, thou art there.
If I take the wings of the morning
and dwell in the uttermost parts of the sea;
Even there shall thy hand lead me,
and thy right hand shall hold me.

Psalms, CXXXIX:2

Sleep, baby, sleep!
Thy rest shall angels keep,
While on the grass the lamb shall feed,
And never suffer want or need.
Sleep, baby, sleep!

Lullaby

Their garments are white, but with an unearthly whiteness. I cannot describe it, because it cannot be compared to earthly whiteness; it is much softer to the eye. These bright Angels are enveloped in a light so different from ours that by comparison everything else seems dark. When you see a band of fifty you are lost in amazement. They seem clothed with golden plates, constantly moving, like so many suns.

Père Lamy

A cherub is God's baby angel
A kiss from heaven.

Leila Murphy

May Cupid's shafts by love
imprest
Smile sweetly soothing in thy breast
Inspiring ardent love for me
As pure and true as mine for thee.

Victorian song

THE LITTLE BOOK OF CHERUBS

Silent, one by one, in the infinite meadows of heaven, blossomed the lovely stars, the forget-me-nots of angels.

Henry Wadsworth Longfellow

And the angel came in unto her, and said, 'Hail, thou that art highly favoured, the Lord is with thee: blessed art thou among women.'

Luke, 1:28

THE LITTLE BOOK OF CHERUBS

And a special angel came down, called a cherub, which is a baby angel. And he rested next to Jesus and they were the same size. Jesus and the cherub shone light, but Jesus was lighter. He was God's son.

Cole, 5

Everything was quiet; everywhere there was the faint
crackling silence of the winter night. We started
singing, and we were all moved by the words
and the sudden trueness of our voices.
Pure, very clear, and breathless, we sang:
As Joseph was a-walking
He heard an angel sing,
'This night shall be the birth-time
Of Christ the Heavenly King.'

Laurie Lee, *Cider with Rosie*

Hush! my dear, lie still and slumber,
Holy angels guard thy bed!
Heavenly blessings without number
Gently falling on thy head.

Isaac Watts, 'Cradle Hymn'

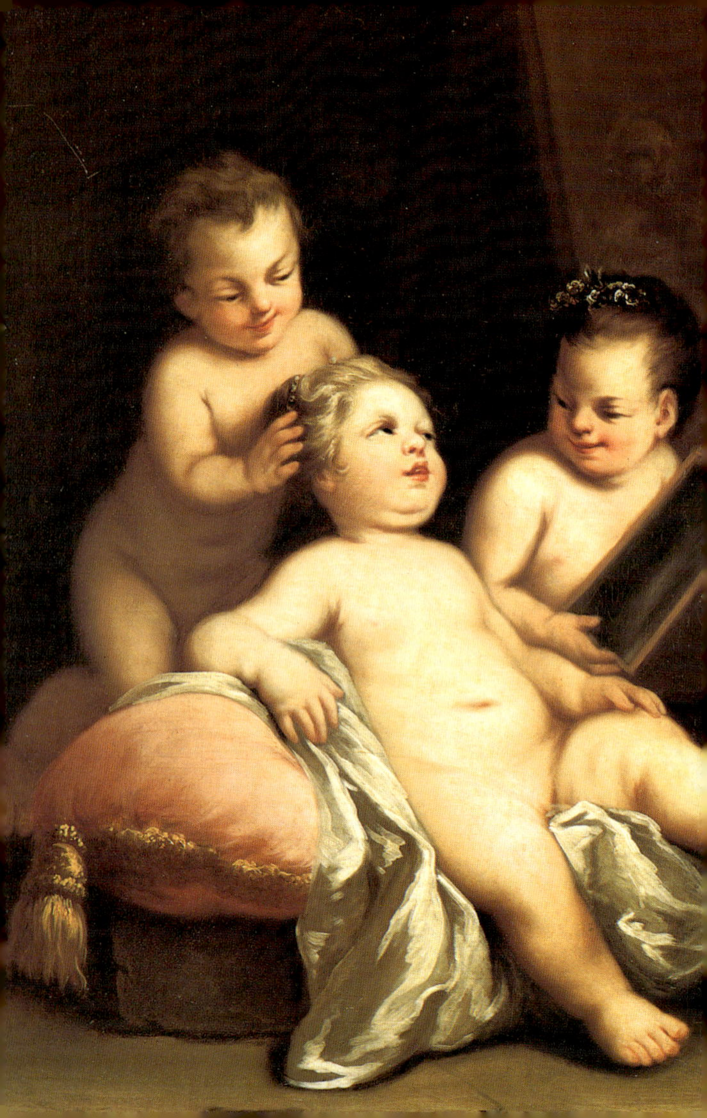

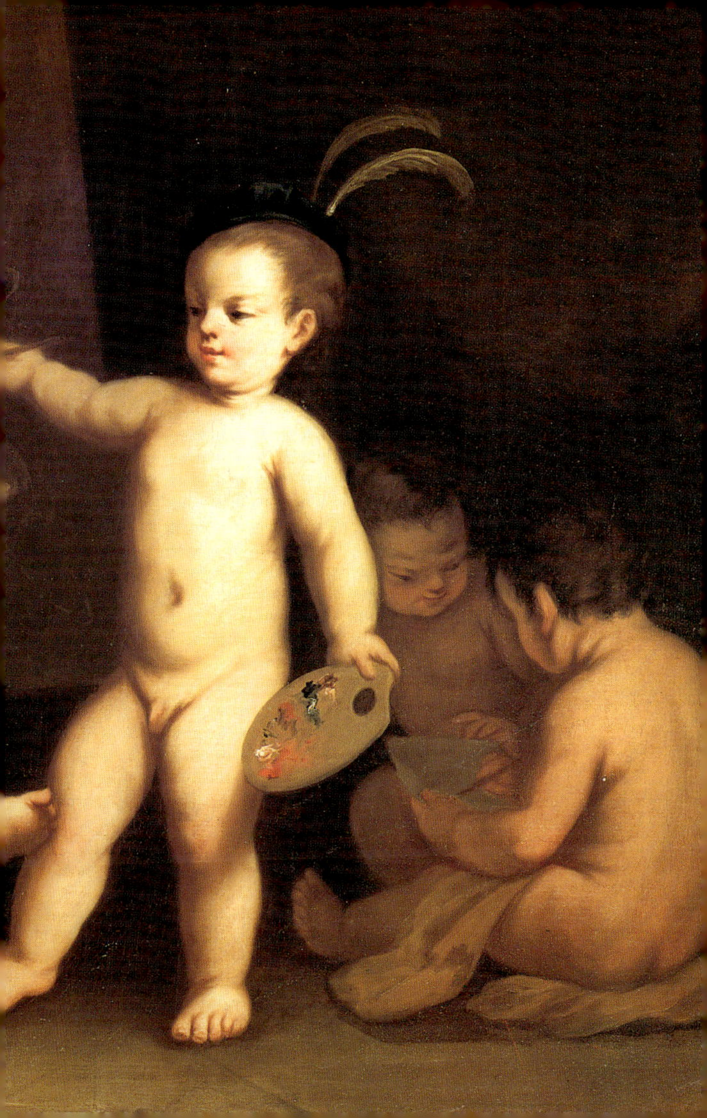

THE LITTLE BOOK OF CHERUBS

The angels are so enamoured of the language that is spoken in heaven, that they will not distort their lips with the hissing and unmusical dialects of men, but speak their own, whether there be any who understand it or not.

Ralph Waldo Emerson

There are nine orders of angels, to wit, angels, archangels, virtues, powers, principalities, dominations, thrones, cherubim, and seraphim.

Pope Gregory the Great

Does the winged life destroy;
But he who kisses the joy as it flies
Lives in Eternity's sunrise.

William Blake

Fears make cherubim of angels; They never see truly.

William Shakespeare

He who binds to himself a joy
Happier of happy though I be, like them
I cannot take possession of the sky,
Mount with a thoughtless impulse, and wheel there,
One of a mighty multitude whose way
And motion is a harmony and dance
Magnificent.

William Wordsworth

And lo, the angel of the Lord came upon them,
and the glory of the Lord shone round about them:
and they were sore afraid.
And the angel said unto them,
'Fear not: for, behold, I bring you good tidings
of great joy, which shall be to all people.
For unto you is born this day in the city of David
a Saviour, which is Christ the Lord.'

Luke, II:9—11

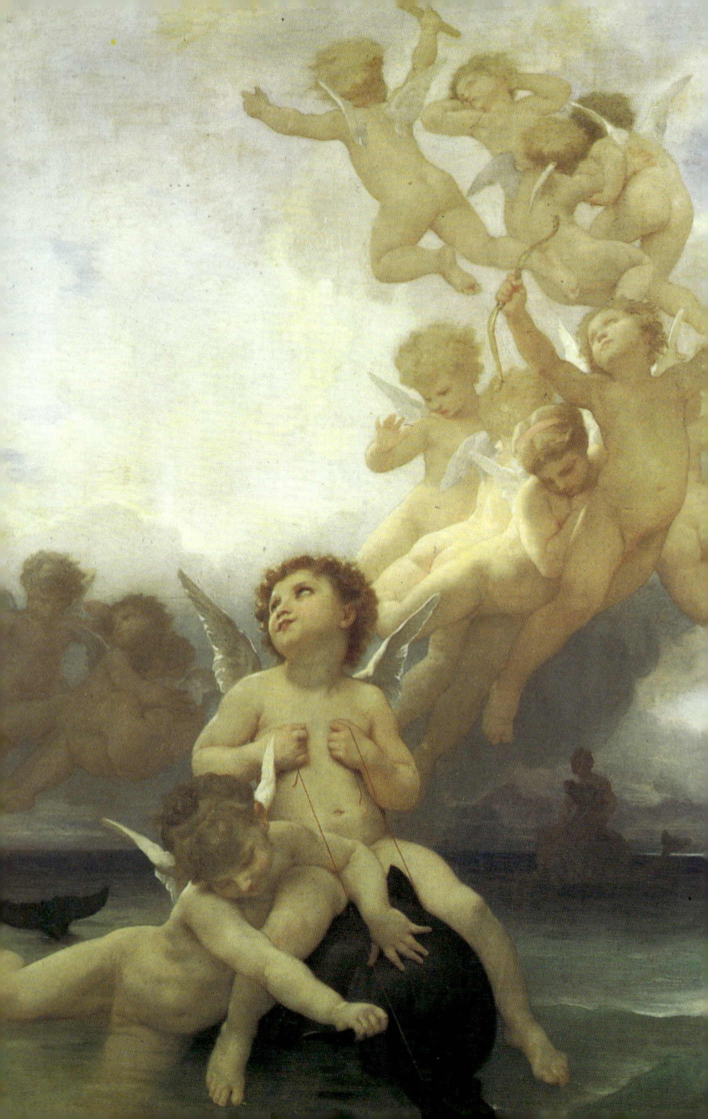

THE LITTLE BOOK OF CHERUBS

Flowers have spoken to me more than I can tell in written words. They are the hieroglyphics of angels, loved by all men for the beauty of the character, though few can decipher even fragments of their meaning.

Lydia M. Child

It is not known precisely where angels dwell — whether in the air, the void, or the planets. It has not been God's pleasure that we should be informed of their abode.

Voltaire

In Heaven an angel is nobody in particular.

George Bernard Shaw

The soul can split the sky in two,
And let the face of God shine through.

Edna St Vincent Millay

A cherub is a firefly.

Luke, 3

In both Judaic and Christian lore, God is said to have stationed 'East of Eden the Cherubim and the Ever Turning Sword to guard the way to the Tree of Life'.

Malcolm Godwin, *Angels*

'Cherub' means 'Knowledge'. In the original Hebrew form they were the bearers of God's Throne, awesome beings with four wings and faces. John of Patmos, in the *Book of Revelations*, insists, however, that they have six wings and six faces.

Sleep, little Baby, sleep;
The holy Angels love thee,
And guard thy bed, and keep
A blessed watch above thee.
No spirit can come near
Nor evil beast to harm thee:
Sleep, Sweet, devoid of fear
Where nothing need alarm thee.

The Love which doth not sleep,
The eternal Arms surround thee:
The Shepherd of the sheep
In perfect love hath found thee.
Sleep through the holy night,
Christ-kept from snare and sorrow,
Until thou wake to light
And love and warmth to-morrow.

Christina Rossetti, 'Holy Innocents'

THE LITTLE BOOK OF CHERUBS

THE LITTLE BOOK OF CHERUBS

THE LITTLE BOOK OF CHERUBS

Enjoy the Spring of Love and Youth,
To some good angel leave the rest;
For Time will teach thee soon the truth,
There are no birds in last year's nest!

Henry Wadsworth Longfellow

Gentle Jesus, meek and mild,
Look upon a little child;
Pity my simplicity,
Suffer me to come to thee.

Charles Wesley

Then when I am thy captive talk of chains,
Proud limitary cherub.

John Milton, *Paradise Lost*

Holy, Holy, Holy! all the saints adore thee,
Casting down their golden crowns
around the glassy sea,
Cherubim and Seraphim falling down before thee,
Which wert, and art, and evermore shalt be.

Reginald Heber, 'Hymn'

A skylark wounded in the wing —
A cherubim does cease to sing.

William Blake, 'Auguries of Innocence'

There was once an angel. This angel was a good angel.
She prayed to God. She never tripped you over.
She did nice things.

Alex, 5

Every blade of grass has its Angel that bends over it
and whispers, 'Grow, grow.'

The Talmud

The helmèd cherubim
And sworded seraphim
Are seen in glittering ranks with wings displayed.

John Milton, 'On the Morning of Christ's Nativity'

How sweet the moonlight sleeps upon this bank!
Here will we sit, and let the sounds of music
Creep in our ears: soft stillness and the night
Become the touches of sweet harmony.
Sit, Jessica: look, how the floor of heaven
Is thick inlaid with patinas of bright gold:
There's not the smallest orb which thou behold'st
But in his motion like an angel sings,
Still quiring to the young-eyed cherubins.

William Shakespeare, *The Merchant of Venice*

But if she sang or if she spoke,
'Twas music soft and grand,
As though a distant singing sea
Broke on a tuneful strand;
As though a blessed Angel were singing a glad song,
Halfway between earth and heaven.

Christina Rossetti

Immortal cherubims! And young men glittering
and sparkling angels, and maids strange seraphic pieces
of life and beauty!

Thomas Traherne, 'Centuries of Meditations'

Angels, from the realms of glory,
Wing your flight o'er all the earth,
Ye who sang creation's story,
Now proclaim Messiah's birth
Come and worship,
Worship Christ the new-born King.

James Montgomery

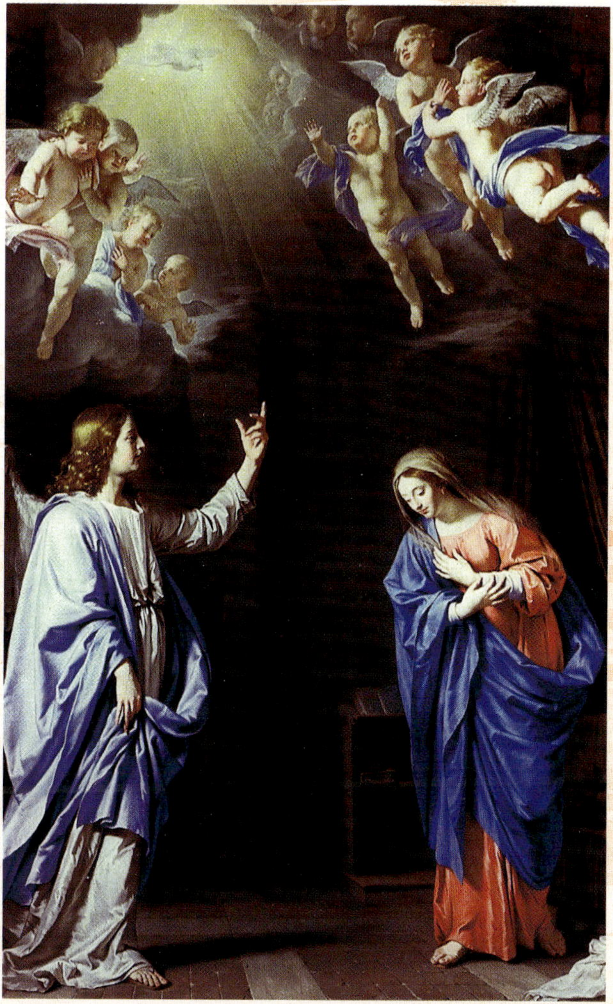

THE LITTLE BOOK OF CHERUBS

Angels shine from without because their spirits are lit
from within by the light of God.

Country lore

Once upon a time there was a little good angel, and she
was a good angel. One day she flew around in the
house and the next day she went to get some food to
eat tomorrow. And she had a lovely time.

Libby, 5

Birds on box and laurels listen,
As so near the cherubs hymn.

Christopher Smart, 'Hymns and Spiritual Songs'

Now all the Angels of the Lord,
Rise up on Christmas Even:
The passing night will hear the Word
That is the voice of Heaven.
Sing sweet as the flute,
Sing clear as the horn,
Sing joy of the Angels,
Come Christmas the Morn:
Little Christ Jesus Our brother is born.

Eleanor Farjeon

The fair creature came towards us, clothed in white and such in his face as seems the tremulous morning star. He opened his arms and then spread his wings and said, 'Come: the steps are at hand here, and henceforth the climb is easy.'

Dante, *The Divine Comedy*, 'Purgatory'

THE LITTLE BOOK OF CHERUBS

Who, if I cried out, would heed me amid
the host of the Angels?

Rainer Maria Rilke, 'The Duino Elegies'

Two thousand times of snow declare
That on the Christmas of the year
There is a-singing in the air;
And all who listen for it hear
A fairy chime, a seraph strain,
Telling He is born again,
That all we love is born again.

James Stephens

Angels and archangels
May have gathered there,
Cherubim and seraphim Thronged the air;
But only his mother
In her maiden bliss
Worshipped the Beloved With a kiss.

Christina Rossetti, 'In The Bleak Mid-Winter'

THE LITTLE BOOK OF CHERUBS

And when, in the darkness of the Scuola di San Rocco in Venice, the angel of the Annunciation bursts like a projectile into Mary's chamber, a shower of putti in his wake, you will positively shiver at
the mighty wind they create.

Gottfried Knapp,

Angels, Archangels, and All the Company of Heaven

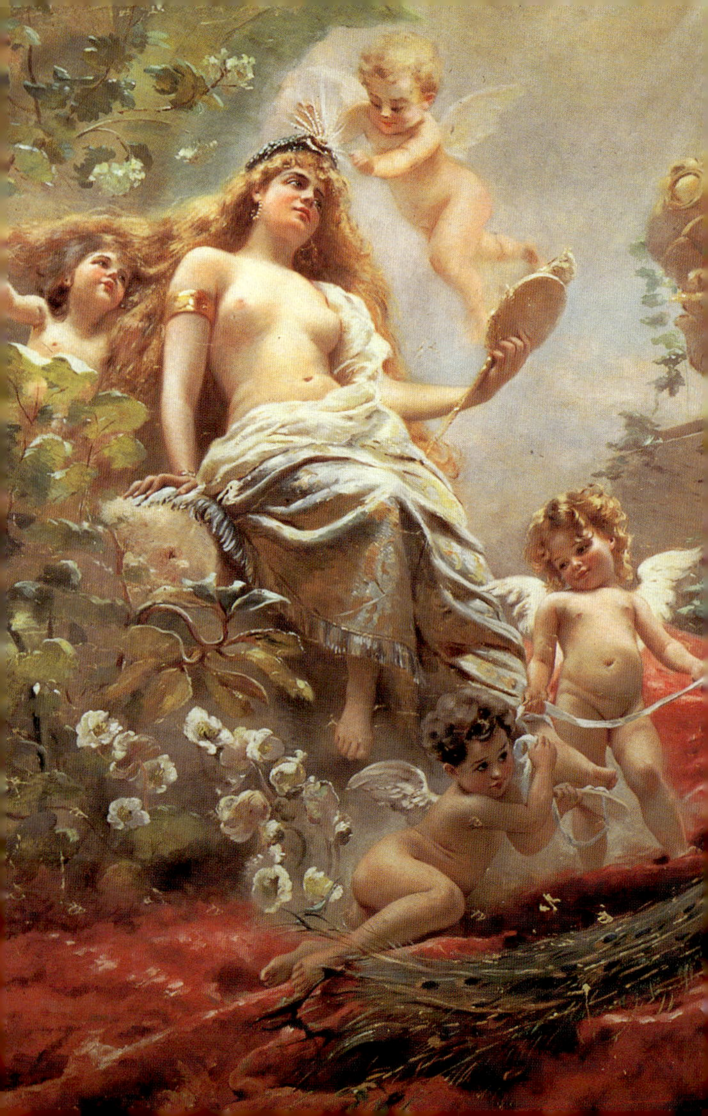

THE LITTLE BOOK OF CHERUBS

And at the midpoint, with outstretched wings, I saw more than a thousand angels making festival, each one distinct in effulgence and in ministry.

Dante, *The Divine Comedy*

Now tell the poor young children, O my brothers,
　　To look up to Him and pray;
So the blessèd One who blesseth all the others,
　　Will bless them another day.
They answer, 'Who is God that He should hear us,
　　While the rushing of the iron wheels is stirred?
When we sob aloud, the human creatures near us
　　Pass by, hearing not, or answer not a word.
And we hear not (for the wheels in their resounding)
　　Strangers speaking at the door:
Is it likely God, with angels singing round Him,
　　Hears our weeping any more?...'

Elizabeth Barrett Browning,
'The Cry of The Children'

May loving angels guard and keep thee,
ever pure as thou art now.

Victorian love message

THE LITTLE BOOK OF CHERUBS

THE LITTLE BOOK OF CHERUBS

Mohammed said that every raindrop that falls is accompanied by an Angel — for even a raindrop is a manifestation of being. The Angelic World is a place inhabited by living creatures — but more than that, it constitutes the very relationship between the world and God.

The Little Book of Angels

There's not the smallest orb which thou behold'st
But in his motion like an angel sings.

William Shakespeare, *The Merchant of Venice*

Have We not made the earth as a cradle
and the mountains as pegs?
And We created you in pairs,
and We appointed your sleep for a rest;
and We appointed night for a garment,
and We appointed day for a livelihood.
And We have built above you seven strong ones,
and We appointed a blazing lamp
and have sent down
out of the rain-clouds water cascading
that We may bring forth thereby grain and plants,
and gardens luxuriant.

The Qur'an

What is it that makes the two putti in the *Sistine Madonna* so irresistible? Is it the naughtiness of the Terrible Twins declining to cavort appropriately among the clouds and curtains, preferring to loll about on the lower border of the picture?

Gottfried Knapp, *Angels, Archangels, and All the Company of Heaven*

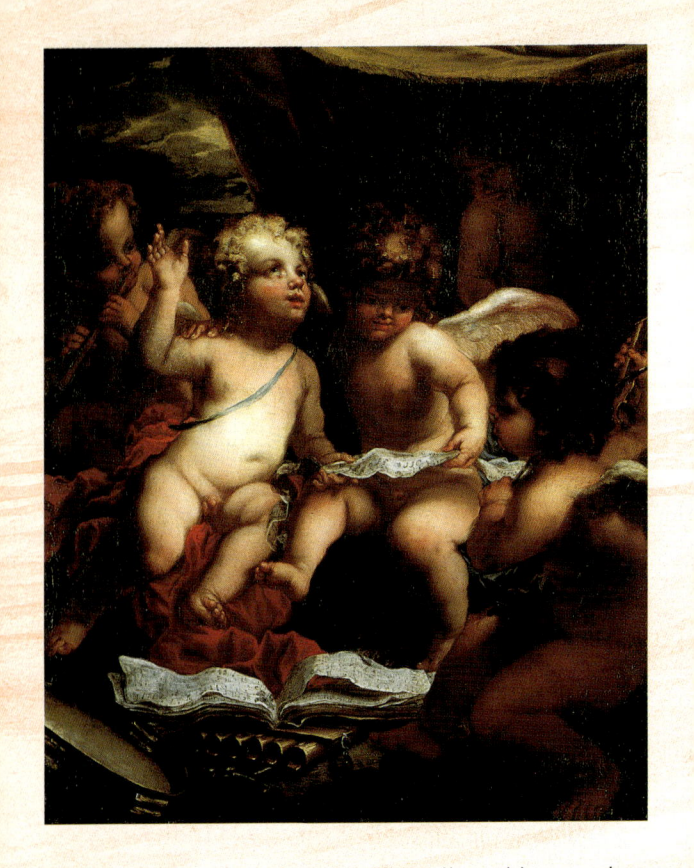

The Lord, before whom I walk, will send his angel
with you and make your way successful.

Genesis, XXIV:40

In this dim world of clouding cares,
We rarely know, till 'wildered eyes
See white wings lessening up the skies
The angels with us unawares.

Gerald Massey, 'Ballad of Babe Christabel'

Around our pillows golden ladders rise,
And up and down the skies,
With winged sandals shod.
The angels come, and go, the Messengers of God.

Richard Henry Stoddard, 'Hymn to the Beautiful'

...it was the angels who uplifted our illustrious ancestors towards the divine, and they did so by prescribing roles of conduct, by turning them from wandering and sin to the right way of truth, or by coming to announce and explain sacred orders, hidden vision or transcendent mysteries, or divine prophecies.

Dionysius

Of sunbeams, shadows, butterflies, and birds
Angels and winged creatures that are lords
Without restraint of all which they behold.

William Wordsworth, 'Home at Grasmere'

Angels at the foot,
And Angels at the head,
And like a curly little lamb
My pretty babe in bed.

Christina Rossetti

When a man opens his heart, for even an instant, the figure he perceives (or the intuition he receives) is his Guardian Angel. When he hears the call to the spiritual life, when his psychic substance is protected from evil, when he meets certain mysterious figures in dreams, or even in waking day, who act out for him the drama of his own inner life —
this is the Guardian Angel at work.

The Little Book of Angels

le 10
Vandemiere
an 6.

THE LITTLE BOOK OF CHERUBS

THE LITTLE BOOK OF CHERUBS

...And now 'twas like all instruments,
Now like a lonely flute;
And now it is an angel's song,
That makes the heavens be mute.

Samuel Taylor Coleridge

And above the glorious crescendo of sound that was the sound of angels, was a tinkle of the heartstrings. The cherubim on high.

Daphne Traitor

Can love be controlled by advice?
Will Cupid our mothers obey?
Though my heart were as frozen as ice,
At his flame 'twould have melted away.
When he kissed me so closely he pressed,
'Twas so sweet that I must have complied:
So I thought it both safest and best
To marry, for fear you should chide.

John Gay

And yet, as angels in some brighter dreams
Call to the soul when man doth sleep,
So some strange thoughts
transcend our wonted themes,
And into glory peep.

Henry Vaughan

Where can the postman be, I say?
he ought to fly — on such a day!
Of all days in the year, you know,
It's monstrous rude to be so slow:
The fellow's so exceeding stupid —
Hark! — there he is! oh! the dear CUPID!

Victorian rhyme

...That while you, I thus recall
From your sleep, I solely,
Me from mine an angel shall,
With reveille holy.

Elizabeth Barrett Browning

THE LITTLE BOOK OF CHERUBS

THE LITTLE BOOK OF CHERUBS

Still through the cloven skies they come,
With peaceful wings unfurled;
And still their heavenly music floats
O'er all the weary world;
Above its sad and lonely plains
They bend on hovering wing;
And ever o'er its Babel sounds
The blessed angels sing.

Edmund Hamilton Sears,
'It Came Upon the Midnight Clear'

How fading are the joys we dote upon!
Like apparitions seen and gone.
But those which soonest take their flight
Are the most exquisite and strong —
Like angels' visits, short and bright;
Mortality's too weak to bear them long.

John Norris, 'The Parting'

And now, if you open the window, look out into the night sky, and listen very carefully, perhaps you will hear the fluttering of myriad pairs of tiny wings...

Gottfried Knapp,

Angels, Archangels, and All the Company of Heaven

The glorious image of the Maker's beauty,
My sovereign saint, the idol of my thought,
Dare not henceforth above the bounds of duty
T'accuse of pride, or rashly blame for aught.
For, being as she is divinely wrought,
And of the brood of angels heavenly born,
And with the crew of blessed saints upbrought,
Each of which did her with their gifts adorn,
The bud of joy, the blossom of the morn,
The beam of light, whom mortal eyes admire,
What reason is it then but she should scorn
Base things, that too her love too bold aspire?
Such heavenly forms ought rather worshipped be,
Than dare be loved by men of mean degree.

Edmund Spenser

THE LITTLE BOOK OF CHERUBS

THE LITTLE BOOK OF CHERUBS

Look for me in the nurseries of heaven.
Francis Thompson

I love to hear the story
Which angel voices tell.
Emily Miller, 'The Little Corporal'

Therefore with Angels, and Archangels, and with all
the company of heaven, we laud and magnify
thy glorious Name, evermore praising thee,
and saying: Holy, holy, holy, Lord God of Hosts,
heaven and earth are full of thy glory:
Glory be to thee, O Lord most High. Amen.
Prayer Book, 'Hymn of Praise'

Open your heart, cherub
You are my light, cherub
And I am your's.
Anonymous

Notes on Illustrations

Pages 6-7 *A Heavenly Trio* by Hans Zatzka. Courtesy of Christie's Images. **Page 8** *The Rest on the Flight into Egypt with Putti Bearing Fruit and Disporting* by Adriaen Van Nieulandt. Courtesy of Christie's Images. **Page 11** *The Glorification of a Bishop Saint* by Girolamo Pesci. Courtesy of Christie's Images. **Page 12** *Detail: Rest on the Return from Egypt* by Jan Brueghal II, Hendrick van Balen. Courtesy of Christie's Images. **Page 15** *L'Enlevement d'Europe* by Boucher (Louvre, Paris). Courtesy of Visual Arts Library. **Page 16** *Portrait of the Right Honourable William Lamb as a Child* by Maria Cosway. Courtesy of Christie's Images. **Pages 18-19** *Putti as Apelles and Campaspe* by Jacopo Amigoni. Courtesy of Christie's Images. **Page 20** *Putti Disporting* by Constantin Jegorowitsch Makowsky. Courtesy of Christie's Images. **Page 22** *The Birth of Venus* by William Adolphe Bougereau. Courtesy of Christie's Images. **Page 24** *Les Forges de Vulcain* by Boucher (Musée de Louvre, Paris). Courtesy of Visual Arts Library. **Pages 26-7** *Spring* by Boucher (The Wallace Collection, London). Courtesy of Visual Arts Library. **Page 28** *Putti with Lions and a Chariot* by a follower of Sir Peter Paul Rubens. Courtesy of Christie's Images. **Page 30** *Water: Putti Blowing Bubbles* by Hendrik Willem Schweickhardt. Courtesy of Christie's Images. **Page 33** *The Annunciation* by Philippe de Champaigne (The Wallace Collection, London). Courtesy of Visual Arts Library. **Page 34** *Venus Mourning Adonis* by G. de Lairesse (Private Collection). Courtesy of Visual Arts Library. **Page 37** *Infant Bacchus, Portrait of the Honourable George Lamb* by Maria Cosway. Courtesy of Christie's Images. **Pages 38-9** *The Toilet of Venus* by Constantin Makowsky. Courtesy of Christie's Images. **Page 40** *Putti Artists* by Stefano Magnasco. Courtesy of Christie's Images. **Pages 42-3** *Venus Lighting Cupid's Torch* attributed to Etienne Jeaurat. Courtesy of Christie's Images. **Page 44** *Three Cherubs* by a follower of B. Luini. Courtesy of Christie's Images. **Page 46** *Putti Musicians* by Stefano Magnasco. Courtesy of Christie's Images. **Page 49** *Cupid Commemorating a Marriage by Incising on a Tablet* by Jean-Baptiste Huet. Courtesy of Christie's Images. **Pages 50-1** *The Triumph of Venus* attributed to Etienne Jeaurat. Courtesy of Christie's Images. **Pages 54-5** *Une Allegorie des Arts* by Charles Eisen. Courtesy of Christie's Images. **Pages 58-9** *Putti Frolicking in the Clouds* by Charles Chaplin. Courtesy of Christie's Images.

Acknowledgements: The Publishers wish to thank everyone who gave permission to reproduce the quotes in this book. Every effort has been made to contact the copyright holders, but in the event that an oversight has occurred, the publishers would be delighted to rectify any omissions in future editions of this book. Children's quotes printed courtesy of Herne Hill School; George Bernard Shaw reprinted courtesy of the Society of Authors on behalf of the Estate of George Bernard Shaw; Laurie Lee, *Cider with Rosie*, reprinted by permission of Andre Deutsch and Penguin Books, and Peters, Fraser & Dunlop Group Ltd; extracts from *The Little Book of Angels*, reprinted courtesy of Element Books; Gottfried Knapp, in *Angels, Archangels and All the Company of Heaven*, reprinted courtesy of Prestel; *Angels*, James Underhill, reprinted courtesy of Element Books Limited © Sean Konecky 1994; *The Angel's Little Instruction Book*, extracts reprinted courtesy of Marshall Pickering, an imprint of HarperCollins Publishers.